SKYE:

CW00922407

A Postcard Tour

Bob Charnley & Roger Miket

Maclean Press, 60 Aird Bhearnasdail, by Portree, Isle of Skye. Tel: 047 042 309

© **1992** Bob Charnley & Roger Miket   ISBN 0 9516022 2 5
Concept, design and layout by **Maclean Press**
Photographic reproduction : Neil Gerrard
Second Edition 1995
Printed by Adlard Print & Typesetting Services, The Old School, The Green,
Ruddington, Notts. NG11 6HH

CONTENTS

INTRODUCTION

The photographs contained within these pages were taken by a variety of cameramen visiting Skye between the early 1860s and the late 1930s. The finished product was sold, either as an original sepia photograph for pasting into a Victorian photograph album, or as a picture postcard, especially for the Edwardian postcard album. The selection has been mine; the illustrations within this book are some of my own favourites, chosen from a personal collection of some 7,000 images of the Scottish islands. The captions, which offer a little of the background to each, are due virtually to the single-handed efforts of Roger. Together they will give an interesting, and hopefully informative, impression of the island as seen by the visitor two and more generations ago.

Treat this offering as an item of nostalgia. Visit as many of the places as you are able, and take your own photographs as a record for future generations, but most of all enjoy the splendour of Skye, and do remember to send a postcard to the family and friends back at home!

Bob Charnley

A Brief History of the British Picture Postcard

The private picture postcard was introduced to the public in Britain in September, 1894. Before that date, a Briton might *receive* illustrated postcards from abroad, but his own reply, from within the United Kingdom, was restricted to those *plain* postcards, or postal stationery, as sold by the Post Office from the year 1870 onward; dull pieces of card, with a pre-printed stamp, used primarily for business purposes. The '*Address Only*' was restricted to the stamp side of the card, with the message on the other, "*Messrs. Jones and Son are pleased to inform you that their representative, Mr Smith, will be in your area on Thursday next, and will be honoured to accept your esteemed order*".

The actual size of those first, privately produced picture postcards, or 'Court Cards' as they were known, was small (4.5 x 3.5 inches) and strictly controlled, as was the length of the message one could write for the halfpenny postage rate. Over five words and the Post Office deemed it to be letter, and surcharged the recipient 1d if the sender ignored the regulations! Hence the origin of those *"Wish you were here. Flossie."* and *"Weather fine, food good. Alf"* type of messages. As these communications had to be written on the picture side, all the early postcards had small illustrations, more often line drawings rather than photographic images, surrounded by a large area of empty space.

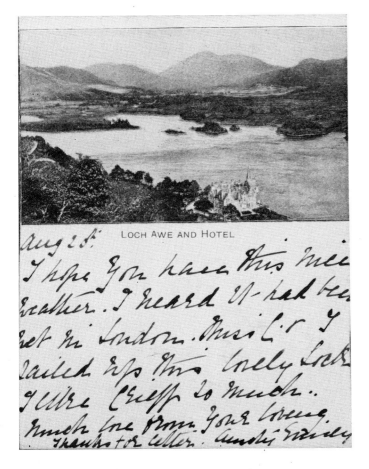

LOCH AWE AND HOTEL

'Court Card', at actual size.
[Valentine Series]

In 1899, the Post Office permitted the postcard to be increased to what would be the standard size, 5.5 x 3.5 inches, but other restrictions were retained for a further three years. In October, 1902, the new full-illustration postcards, with plenty of space *next* to the address for a longer message, were introduced, and the words, *"Address Only on this Side"*, became obsolete. Publishers could now divide the stamp-side of the card with a line down the middle, so as to accommodate both message and the address. This, in turn, freed the picture side of the postcard, and the whole area was now made available for an amazing selection of photographs and original art-work. The craze for collecting postcards swept the country!

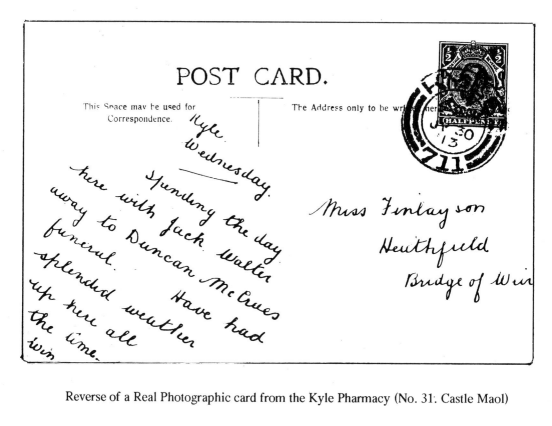

Reverse of a Real Photographic card from the Kyle Pharmacy (No. 31: Castle Maol)

Official returns from the Post Office show just how popular this form of pre-telephone communication was. In 1895 some 313 million postcards passed through our postal system, and it has been estimated that just 30% were the new, private picture postcards (see 'Collecting Picture Postcards - an Introduction' by A. Byatt. 1982). In 1902 the figure was 445 million, but by 1912 it had doubled to 905 million postcards, and now the *picture* postcard dominated the market, the estimated figure in its favour being 90%, with the official, *plain* Post Office card struggling to survive.

In 1918 the postcard rate was increased to 1d, pushed to one-and-a-half pence in 1921, and reduced down to 1d again, in under 12 months, simply because of customer resistance. But by this time the postcard had lost ground to the telephone, as an efficient, quick method of communication, and the sale of cards became more seasonal, with summer holidaymakers being the main users.

And it was the summer tourist, visiting Skye and other Scottish isles, who purchased many of the more interesting, photographic images of the Hebrides that were taken between 1920 and the outbreak of World War 11 in 1939. Reproduced as postcards, one of the very best series was published by an English firm, the *Scholastic Souvenir Company* of Bispham, Blackpool, and a few of their Skye postcards are sprinkled throughout this book.

Various trade-marks were used by the firm to identify their cards, but, in common with many other publishers, the *Scholastic Souvenir Company* failed to mark all of the postcards, and many examples of their work still lie, unrecognised, in albums and old cardboard boxes throughout the country. None of the many postcard reference works mention this particular firm, but in 1984 I undertook some research into the history of the *Scholastic Souvenir Company*, and an article subsequently appeared in a private, small-circulation magazine called '*Delta*', the newsletter of the Red Rose Postcard Club based in Lancashire. Briefly, this is just a small part of the story behind those *Scholastic Souvenir Company* postcards.

In the Yorkshire mill town of Hebden Bridge, in the year 1900, lived Mr. Willie Binns, a sickly young man who suffered from a tubercular hip which brought him prolonged periods of confinement. Such adversity kept him from the mill, with the subsequent loss of income, and forced him into seeking some form of less arduous, but regular, employment. Being a keen amateur photographer, he decided to exploit the market in school-group photographs; thus the *Scholastic Souvenir Company* was founded with the young Mr. Binns as sole owner.

Year in and year out he visited his local schools, taking individual or class photographs on request, then producing the prints in his own dark-room and selling them to the parents at a cost of either 6d or 1/-. The work was steady but Willie's health was not, and his doctor advised him to move to the coast if he wished to prolong his life. And so, in 1917, the Binns family left the security of their Yorkshire home to settle in Bispham, a small village close to the Lancashire sea-side resort of Blackpool.

Here the business flourished, and Willie was able to expand his territory, and he set about recruiting freelance photographers throughout the British Isles. They were to find the schools in their location, take the photographs, and post the unexposed film or glass plates, to Blackpool, where Willie undertook the developing and printing work. In return they received commission on the sales generated by the photographs. In few instances did it provide full-time employment for the photographer, but it was an opportunity for disabled war veterans or, particularly, commercial travellers, to supplement their incomes as they moved regularly between one town, or island, and another.

But in the long summer months, when schools were closed and work was scarce, the need for a source of income still remained as a priority. Since all the records of the company were destroyed in the 1950s, it is not possible to say who thought of the idea in the first instance, but one of the commercial travellers may well have been asked, by a local shopkeeper or postmaster in the Hebrides, to produce a '*new*' postcard view for the summer visitors. Some of the very earliest *Scholastic Souvenir* cards in the collection come from the islands, and include views of Castlebay, in beautiful Barra, and Tiree, in the Inner Hebrides. The larger publishers of postcards, Valentine's and Tuck's for example, were not interested in 'small orders' for 100 view-cards of a local hotel, but this was exactly the type of business that Willie Binns and his *Scholastic Souvenir Company* could handle with ease, and he grasped his opportunity.

Scholastic Souvenir Co., Bispham, Blackpool.

In the mid 1920s the IVth year pupils at Portree High School sit for their class photograph by the 'Scholastic Souvenir Co. Bispham, Blackpool'. Perhaps when they return to their lessons the photographer will take the opportunity to take a few landscape or 'character' photographs back with him to see if Mr Binns might consider them worthy as postcard views? [With thanks to the Portree History Society for permission to reproduce this photograph]

In 1928, Harry, the eldest son in the Binns' household, joined the company and the future appeared secure for the family-run business, but the war intervened and Harry joined the RAF. And then, tragedy! In 1941 he was reported missing, *'believed killed in action'*, over the English Channel; the aircraft, in which he was the Observer, failed to return from a bombing mission.

The war had already curtailed the postcard side of the business by the early days of 1940, and with the peace Willie Binns made the decision that it should not be started up again. He died in 1958 and control of the 'school-photographs-only' business, passed to his daughter Marjorie, now Mrs. Rhodes, who continues to operate the *Scholastic Souvenir Company* today. Sadly, no records, *except one,* survive from the early years of the company through to 1939. All the glass plates, celluloid negatives, sample postcards, order-forms, records, and names of Willie's photographers, were deliberately destroyed; they represented a lost generation, and the space they occupied was more important than sentiment.

But the one surviving link with the past is, appropriately enough, an old black and white photograph. Discovered within the works, in the drawer of a desk, it shows the mail-room of the *Scholastic Souvenir Company* sometime in the mid-1930s. A vast quantity of new postcards are ready for wrapping and dispatch, whilst parcels, some addressed to outlets in the Isle of Man and Tarbert, Harris, are ready for delivery to the G.P.O. Can any doubt the success of Willie Binns' business upon seeing this picture from the past?

Today, the postcard trade still flourishes, although most of the 'big names', from those early years, have long gone. The collector of modern, current, postcards, tends to buy thematic cards, whilst the collector of pre-1939 examples veers toward the nostalgic, topographical postcard. A particular modern favourite, the Teddy Bear, is a good example, but the list includes politics, transport, glamour and pop-stars. Many 'postcard-only' fairs are held, at very regular intervals, in towns and cities throughout the United Kingdom, with a major, international, 4 day event in London each September, and other, 2 or 3-day, fairs in cities such as Glasgow and York. Millions of old postcards are available for sale, and the enthusiastic crowd often queue for hours before the doors open!

Certainly the hobby of collecting the humble postcard has not ended, but the price of *some* of the early postcards has risen above the curren rate of inflation, and whilst you might like to collect postcards of, say, the ill-fated liner 'Titanic', it would *definitely* be cheaper if you concentrated on the type of card illustrated within the pages of this book.

SCOTTISH SCENERY

PHOTOGRAPHED BY

G. W. WILSON & Co., ABERDEEN.

Her Majesty's  Photographers in Scotland.

THIS Series of **PHOTOGRAPHS IN SCOTLAND** (commenced in 1852 by Mr G. W. WILSON) consists of over 5000 different Views, and embraces Pictures in every noteworthy district visited by Tourists, including —

Edinburgh and "Land of Burns and Scott"; Glasgow and the Clyde; Trossachs; Loch Katrine; The Scenery on the Highland Railway from Perth to Inverness; The Caledonian Canal; Oban, Staffa, and Iona; Skye; Loch Maree; Ross-shire; Orkney and Shetland; Aberdeen; Deeside; Balmoral, &c., &c., &c.

A New Series of London, Windsor, English Cathedrals, Castles, and Abbeys, just published.

Since the publication of our last Catalogue, a series of Views in each of the following districts has been issued :—

Arran, Sutherland, Orkney and Shetland, Caithness, Ayrshire, Dumfries, Kirkcudbright, Wigton, Fife, Firth of Clyde, &c., Dunbar, Loch Maree, Loch Fyne, Mull, Alnwick, and Warkworth Castle, &c. Private and State Apartments of Windsor Castle, besides additions to almost the whole of the more popular districts.

Published as **SCRAPS** in **Three Sizes**— as Stereoscopic Slides on Glass and Paper ; Magic Lantern Slides ; and Cartes-de-Visite. **SMALL COLLECTIONS** —Forming interesting Souvenirs of the various districts, bound in Green Cloth or Morocco, price from 5s. to £2, 2s.; also **GENERAL TOUR THROUGHOUT SCOTLAND**, containing from 50 to 200 Views, handsomely bound in Best Morocco. Price from £3, 12s. to £10, 10s.

NOVELTY OF THE SEASON—**MEDALLIONS**—in which style most of the above-named can be had.

Sold by Book and Print Sellers, and by Agents on all the Tourist Routes.

CATALOGUES FREE ON APPLICATION.

Advertisement for George Washington Wilson's photographic 'Views', in the 1882 edition of 'Paterson's Tourist Hand-Guide to Scotland'.

PHOTOGRAPHS OF SCOTTISH SCENERY.

G. W. WILSON & CO., ABERDEEN (Photographers to Her Majesty in Scotland), beg to call the attention of Tourists and others visiting Scotland to their lately published

'TOURS IN SCOTLAND,'

Consisting of Sets of Photographs in various bindings, at prices ranging from 12s. to £10, 10s.

Subjoined is a List of Districts in Stock, and special Districts and Sizes can be prepared to order:—Aberdeen—Deeside—Aberdeen and Deeside—Dunkeld, Killiecrankie, and Blair Athole—Land of Burns—Edinburgh—Edinburgh and Land of Scott—Edinburgh, Stirling, and Trossachs—Glasgow and Clyde—Inverness and Caledonian Canal—From Dingwall to Skye—Skye—Orkney—Shetland—Orkney and Shetland—Oban—Oban, Staffa, and Iona—Glencoe--Loch Awe and Dalmally—West Highlands—Trossachs and Loch Katrine—Loch Katrine and Loch Lomond—Aberfeldy, Kenmore, and Killin—Souvenir of Sir Walter Scott.

GENERAL TOUR THROUGHOUT SCOTLAND.

G. W. W. & Co. publish also the largest selection of Photographs of Scottish Scenery, comprising Views on the principal Tourist Routes, in Imperial, Cabinet, and $4\frac{1}{2} \times 3\frac{1}{4}$ Scraps, Stereographs on Glass or Paper, and Cartes-de-Visite. Sold by all Booksellers and Printsellers, and by Agents in the various districts which the Views illustrate. *Catalogues on application.*

PHOTOGRAPHS OF SCOTTISH SCENERY,

BY

J. VALENTINE,

<table>
<tr><td>PHOTOGRAPHER BY
SPECIAL APPOINTMENT</td><td></td><td>TO HER MAJESTY
THE QUEEN.</td></tr>
</table>

DUNDEE,

Embracing a very large series of the principal places of interest in the Lowlands and Highlands, in IMPERIAL (8×10), CABINET, CARD, and STEREOSCOPIC SIZES.

In reference to a series of these Views the late Earl of Dalhousie presented to the Queen, he wrote as follows:—

'SIR,—I think it due to you, as an artist, to inform you that I had the honour of presenting the set of your Photographs to the Queen, and that Her Majesty was pleased to express her approval of them as works of art.

'Yours truly,

'DALHOUSIE.

'To Mr. James Valentine, Dundee.'

SELECTIONS GEOGRAPHICALLY ARRANGED, made up in Morocco and Clan Tartan Wood Bindings, suitable for Presentation, from £1, 1s. to £10, 10s. each.

Also, Illustrations of the various Tourists' districts, in Cabinet and Card Size. Panoramic Books in neat *Blue* Cloth Bindings.

Catalogues on application.

These Views may be had of all respectable Booksellers and Printsellers; also of Agents in the districts which the Views illustrate.

Advertisements for George Washington Wilson and Valentine of Dundee from 'Miller's Royal Tourist Handbook to the Highlands and Islands' (1877-8). What choice on a single page!

THE ROAD TO THE ISLES

COMING TO SKYE ?

Then plan to include a Tour of the Western Highlands and Islands. Make Skye your Headquarters and from there visit the Holiday Land of your dreams—romance, beauty, tonic air—a land unspoiled and unaltered by the passing years, but modern in its comfort and convenience for the Tourist and Holidaymaker.

The Prince Charlie country is well worth seeing—Skye, Uist, Harris, Lewis, also Mull and Iona and the famed beauty spots of the West Mainland Coast.

Enjoy Golf, Fishing (Sea, Loch and Stream), Tennis, Sailing, Bathing, Hill-Climbing, Hiking amidst the most wonderful scenery in Europe.

WRITE FOR PARTICULARS OF SAILINGS, ETC., TO

DAVID MACBRAYNE LTD.
CLYDE HOUSE, 44 ROBERTSON STREET
GLASGOW, C.2

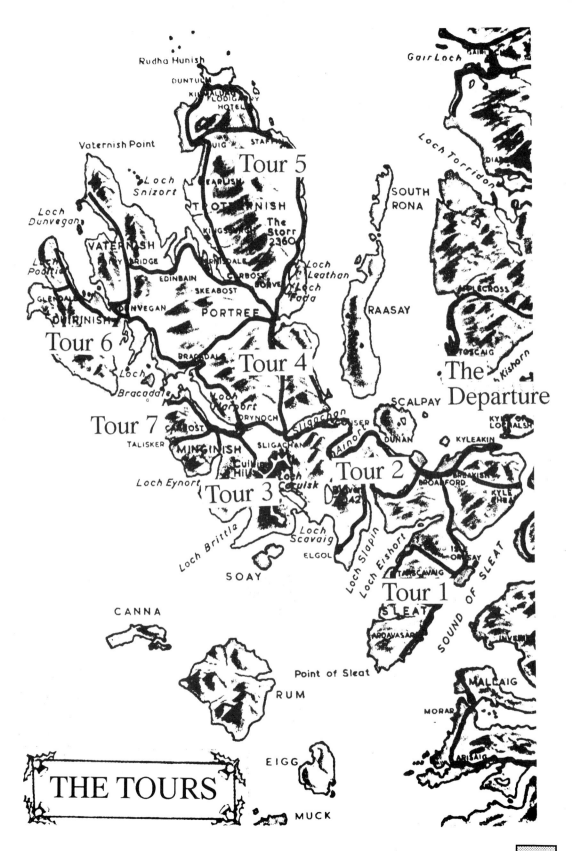

THE TOURS

13

AT EUSTON

Stranger with the pile of luggage proudly labelled for Portree,
How I wish this night of August, I were you and you were me !
Think of all that lies before you when the train goes sliding forth
And the lines athwart the sunset lead you swiftly to the North !
Think of breakfast at Kingussie, think of high Drumochter Pass,
Think of Highland breezes singing through the bracken and the grass,
Scabious blue and yellow daisy, tender fern beside the train,
Rowdy Tummel falling, brawling, seen and lost and glimpsed again !
You will pass my golden roadway of the days of long ago ;
Will you realise the magic of the names I used to know :
Clachnaharry, Achnashellach, Achnasheen, and Duirinish ?
Ev'ry moor alive with coveys, ev'ry pool aboil with fish ?
Ev'ry well-remembered vista more exciting mile by mile
Till the wheeling gulls are screaming round the engine at the Kyle.
Think of cloud on Beinn na Cailleach, jagged Cuchullins soaring high,
Scent of peat and all the glamour of the misty Isle of Skye !

Rods and guncase in the carriage, wise retriever in the van ;
Go, and good luck travel with you ! (Wish I'd half your luck, my man !)

A. M. Harbord.

THE DEPARTURE

KYLE TO KYLEAKIN......

TOURS IN SCOTLAND

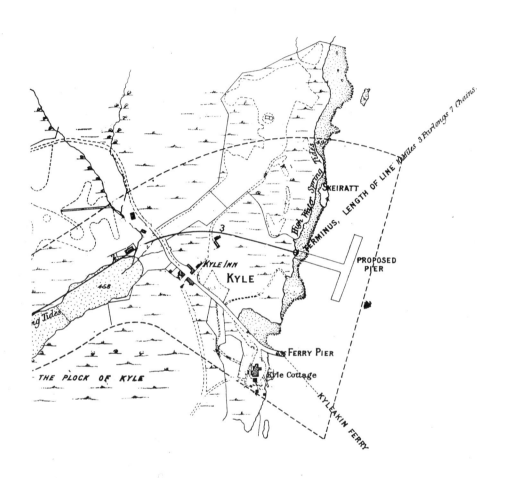

In 1867 Murdoch Paterson was appointed as Engineer to the Skye and Dingwall Railway, rising in 1896 to the position of Engineer-in-Chief. His proposals for a route for the railway from Strome to Kyle were revealed in a series of large-scale plans printed in 1893. Just four years later the railway arrived at Kyle, and with it the popular tourism that fed the burgeoning postcard industry.

1. The station at Kyle of Lochalsh soon after its opening on 2nd November,1897. At the platform is a 'Skye Bogie', a class of engine specially designed by David Jones, Locomotive Superintendent of the Highland Line, to cope with the particularly steep gradients and sharp curves on the route. Although never named, these sturdy workhorses passed into railway legend with the last being built in 1901. The paddle steamer 'Lovedale' (on the right) ran the mail service between Stornoway, Strome Ferry and Kyle at this time, but was scrapped in 1904. [This original sepia photograph bears the mark 'G.W.W' and came from the studio of George Washington Wilson in Aberdeen, although he personally never lived to see this particular station as he died in 1893]

2. Main Street, Kyle of Lochalsh, showing the Commercial Bank to the right and the Kyle Hotel in the centre. Post-cards, (including some from the studio of Washington Wilson) are on sale in the booth on the left. *"I am sending you a deerskin tonight"* writes the sender to Captain Turner at Alma Cottage, Tighnabruaich. *"Trusting you will receive the same alright. We are having rotten weather just now",* he concludes. Not surprising perhaps, for although the postcard depicts a summer scene, it was posted on 18th December,1912. [A hand-tinted postcard from the studio of George Washington Wilson]

Main Street, Kyle Loch Alsh.

3. The Main Street, Kyle of Lochalsh by an anonymous photographer, not too concerned to catch the workmen in the process of building steps giving access to the raised pavement fronting The Bank of Scotland and General Post Office. [Coloured Edwardian postcard which, like many at this time, was, 'Made in Saxony']

The delights of the Kyle Hotel, shown in the above postcard, as advertised in 1906

4. The Station Hotel, Kyle of Lochalsh as it appeared in 1918. Formerly Kyle Cottage, it was renamed when the railway came to Kyle in 1897, and was to undergo a remarkable series of transformations over the following decades. [An early product from the Kyle Pharmacy Series]

5. Lochalsh Hotel. A now very greatly enlarged hotel from that depicted in the previous view, and testifying to the increase of visitors. Described by Iain Anderson in 1934 as, *"The acme of comfort, an L.M.S. Railway Hotel."* Nevertheless, until 1931 the hotel was lit by paraffin lamps and candles. Comfortable bedrooms, and excellent food served in a dining-room with superb views across the Kyle to Skye, make this the perfect base today for a touring holiday of Wester Ross. [Kyle Pharmacy Series]

6. A Real Photographic card sent from Kyle to Master Charles Young at the Moat House, Milbourn, Cambridgeshire. Though the stamp has been removed, no doubt to fill a gap in a junior stamp album, the all-important, unsigned message remains: *"Poor old Frasers Laundry at Kyle of Lochalsh"*. I hope young Master Charles was impressed! [The subject matter and lack of caption indicates this to have been a private picture printed onto photographic paper with a postcard back]

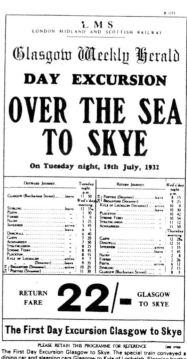

No. 12. KYLE OF LOCHALSH to KYLEAKIN

Across Kyle Akin to Isle of Skye.

Phones   Kyleakin 2 (Night service—Kyleakin 13).   Telegraphic Address :
Ferry, Kyle, Ross-shire.

Two Boats carrying two cars each.   Continuous service for 3 hours before,
and 3 hours after Spring (High) tides ; or 5 to 5½ hours after Neap (High) tides.
Weather and tides permitting, ferry will start at 9 a.m. and finish at dusk from
October to May inclusive ; start 8 a.m. and finish 9 p.m. June, July and
August ; start 8 a.m. and finish 8 p.m. in September. Fairly easy embarkation.
NO SUNDAY SERVICE.

CHARGES :	Single.		Return.	
	s.	d.	s.	d.
Motor-car, up to 12 h.p.	8	0	13	6
,, ,, over 12 h.p.	12	6	20	0
Tri-car	8	0	13	6
Motor Cycle	2	6	4	0
Motor Cycle and Side-car	5	0	8	0
Motor Caravan, up to 12 h.p.	8	0	13	6
,, ,, over 12 h.p.	12	6	20	0
Trailer Caravan	8	0	13	6
Small Luggage Trailer	4	0	6	6
Passengers		6		10

Maximum weight 3 tons 10 cwts.

NOTE.—If a car and trailer can be taken on one journey, the charge for the
trailer is 4s.

From the Automobile Association's 1936 edition of FERRIES in SCOTLAND

7. Be reassured, this postcard depicts an *old* method of reaching Skye by bus! This 14 seater coach bearing a 1928 Glasgow registration GE 1458, has just been 'safely' loaded onto the ferry at Kyle. [Real photographic card]

8. "At the Ferry, Kyle of Lochalsh". The experience of taking such a small craft across the narrows is graphically depicted by Alexander Smith in 1865. *"The ferry is a narrow passage between the mainland and Skye; the current is powerful there, difficult to pull against on gusty days; and the ferryman is loathe to make the attempt unless well remunerated ..... in a short time the boat was ready and the party embarked. The craft was crank and leaked abominably, but there was no help ..... The leak is increasing fast and our bags are well-nigh afloat in the working bilge ..... The llittle Irishwoman, erstwhile so cheery ..... has sunk in a heap at the bow ....."* - They landed safely of course! [Sepia-printed postcard in the 'Kyle Pharmacy Series']

9. The lighthouse at *Eilean Ban* ("Fair island") was built in 1857 and survived as a manned light until 1960. It subsequently became the home of Gavin Maxwell, author of "Ring of Bright Water" and "The Rocks Remain. His vision for an all-Scottish Wildlife Park on the island was cut short by his untimely death in 1969. [Early sepia postcard with the mark 'Munro & Son', posted in 1907.]

10. Kyleakin, Skye. In the late 18th century, various measures were advanced to establish viable industries in the Highlands, usually centred on agriculture or fishing. Hand-in-hand with measures designed to introduce some order and well-being into a society so recently racked by political upheaval, was the impetus towards setting-up townships. These were viewed by Government as a keystone in fostering loyalty to central authority and Highland proprietors were encouraged to establish 'model' villages. In 1811 at the behest of Lord MacDonald, Gillespie Graham designed a new town for Kyleakin which was to be rechristened 'New Liverpool'. It came to nothing, preferring to retain the modest architectural charm it carried into the earliest years of the 20th century. [Tinted, and overprinted with D. MacPherson, Post Office, Kyleakin]

11. The harbour at Kyleakin. To anyone familiar with the location, this is an unlikely setting for the characteristic Edwardian representation of the ever-loved 'man-rows-lady' boating scene. Taken from the ferry landing, this composition shows a number of larger trading vessels, (one beached). These, together with the hotels around the harbour, testify to the increasing volume of visitors since the township was established. [A hand-coloured postcard, *circa* 1904, marked 'Made in Saxony']

12. 'Roderick and Peggy'
[Real photographic card, unattributed]

A HIGHLAND CARGO, KYLEAKIN, SKYE.

13. From the mid-17th century, the Isle of Skye produced black cattle for a growing population in the south. In late summer, great herds would set off from the fairs at Broadford, Dunvegan and Portree along the well-worn droving routes. Until the early decades of the 19th century, the herds were made to swim across the narrows at Kylerhea by towing the lead beast across from a boat and the rest of the herd would follow. By the mid-19th century, the ferry offered a safer alternative. [A Valentine card of 1927, carrying the over-print of J.G. MacKay, Portree]

14. *Caisteal Maol* ('Bare Castle'), Kyleakin, Isle of Skye. This, the first historic monument the visitor to Skye would see as the ferry approached the shore, was built during the first decades of the 16th century by the MacKinnons of Strath. In tradition it was the home of a Scandinavian Princess called 'Saucy Mary', wife of a MacKinnon chief. Her income was said to have been raised from a levy on boats plying the Kyle and to ensure all paid their toll, a chain was stretched across the narrows. Since abandonment in the early 17th century, the structure steadily deteriorated until it was taken into care by the District Council in 1989. [A Black and white postcard from Valentine of Dundee in the early 1900s]

15. On September 11th, 1933, the Duke and Duchess of York landed at Kyleakin *en route* to Portree where they were to officially open the Boys' Hostel for school boarders. The future King, George VI and his Queen are here met at the ferry landing by Major MacKinnon C.M.G. and Alasdair MacDonald of Sleat. The visit was marked by a public holiday. [Real Photographic card by J.B. White of Dundee]

16. Carrying Home the Peats. Traditionally a woman's task. In July 1905, Miss Drummond of Edinburgh was informed by the sender, 'D.F.' that he had seen, *"this today at Kyleakin in Skye almost exactly as photographed."* Twenty years later this card was still popular. [Printed card by Valentine of Dundee]

17. *Eilean Iarmain*, Isle Ornsay Hotel, Sleat. Advertised as "*An old fashioned Highland inn situated on a small private fishing harbour. Open fires and hot water bottles, local Gaelic-speaking staff, and meals based on fresh local ingredients as far as possible, simply cooked. Home-made oatcakes.*" All that has changed here are the cars outside the door! [Unattributed]

18. Armadale Castle, designed by James Gillespie Graham and completed in 1815, was home to the MacDonalds of Sleat. Abandoned after the Second World War, the fabric deteriorated to the extent that in 1969 the 8th Lord MacDonald received permission from Inverness County Council to demolish his former seat. Today this is the focal point for members of Clan Donald everywhere; here you will discover the popular Clan Donald Centre with its 46 acres of woodland gardens, exhibition, with audio-visual theatre, restaurant, bookshop and museum [A black and white printed postcard by Valentine of Dundee with the imprint 'D. MacIntyre, Stationer, Portree, Skye']

Armadale Pier, Skye

19. Armadale Pier.

O' a' the isles o' this braid sea
That noo I navigate
There's nane that in the hert o' me
Looms owre big wi' fate-
Exceptin' Skye.
Gliskin' her crests
Infinite and serene:
Dochter o' God, I cry sich breasts
Are nae for human een
(John Gawsworth).
[Real photographic postcard, 1930s]

"Rates," hints the Automobile Association,
for the Mallaig-Armadale ferry (maximum 4 cars),
"include driver, or if a uniformed chauffeur is em-
ployed the owner will also be carried free." But
there was a sting in the tail on this particular trip!
"Landing charges at Skye: Cars, 1s 4d.: Passen-
gers, 2d."

No. 9. MALLAIG—ARMADALE (SKYE)

Across Sound of Sleat.

Phone : Mallaig 45. Telegraphic Address : Isles Ferry, Mallaig.

Boat carries three or four cars ; the crossing takes about 50 minutes.
Service as required from 8 a.m. till just before dark, from 1st May to early
October. NO SUNDAY SERVICE.

To avoid delay, motorists could wire in advance stating time of arrival
at termini. Loading and unloading at either side over stones and sand,
but this is quite firm.

CHARGES :						Single. £ s. d.	Return. £ s. d.
Cars up to 14 h.p.	...	...	...	...	...	1 0 0	1 15 0
Cars over 14 h.p.	...	...	...	...	...	1 5 0	2 0 0
Tri-cars	...	...	...	...	...	0 15 0	
Motor Cycle	...	...	...	...	...	0 5 0	
Motor Cycle and Side-car	...	...	...	...	0 7 6	

Motor Caravan : up to 30s. single, according to size.

Trailer Caravan : up to 15s. single, according to size.

Small Luggage Trailer : up to 10s. single, according to size.

Above rates include driver, or if a uniformed chauffeur is employed the owner
will also be carried free. Additional passengers, 1s. 6d. single.

Landing charges at Skye : Cars, 1s. 4d. ; Trailers, 6d. ; Motor Cycles, 4d. ;
Passengers, 2d. ; Motor Cycle Combination or Tri-car per ton, 1s. 4d.

Return tickets valid for any period during season.

TO TOURISTS & TRAVELLERS.

THE

SKYE MAIL.

PARTIES travelling in the Isle of Skye will find this a most excellent Conveyance, as it runs Daily between Dunvegan and Kyleakin, in connection with the Mail to and from Dingwall. The Skye Mail departs from the Dunvegan Hotel at 5 a.m., reaches Portree 9 a.m ; leaves there at 9.30 a.m., and arrives at Kyleakin at 3.20 p.m., returning to Portree and Dunvegan on the arrival of the Mail from Dingwall, and calling, going and returning at Sligachan and Broadford.

By the Skye Mail, Tourists are provided with an excellent means of surveying scenery grand, varied, and much admired, as the Route leads through the most romantic scenery in the Island.

Portree, June 21, 1866. JOHN M'KAY.

20. The Ardvasar Hotel as it looked in the early 1930s when this Blackpool-produced postcard was issued. Just a century earlier it had been described as, *"a hovel of one storey,....certainly the most villaneous house in all Scotland for fleas"*. Architecturally the exterior shape has been retained with only the area to the left of the main building altered over the years. But in terms of comfort, what a transformation! [Real photographic postcard by the Scholastic Souvenir Company of Blackpool, *circa* 1933]

21 & 22. In 1863 a post office was established at Ardvasar as the terminus of the mail from Broadford to Sleat. For a brief time the mails were handled from the inn at Ardvasar but by the turn of the century the Kennedy's ran a post office and store from the small corrugated iron building shown in 21. The store continued until the 1980s although by the later 1920s the post office was relocated to the building run by John MacInness shown in 22. In 1982 this too closed and today 'Post Office Counters Ltd.' is run from a neat new bungalow. [Real Photographic postcard, unattributed.]

POST OFFICE, ARDVASAR, SKYE.

TOUR 2 Broadford to Elgol

4067 — A Typical Skye Cottage

23. *"Here and there at long intervals we came to the wretched groups of cottages we had begun to know so well. Old witch-like women and young girls passed, bent double under loads of peat or seaweed, so heavy that were the same thing seen in Italy. English people would long since have filled columns of The Times with their sympathy. As it is, these burdens are accepted as a matter of course, or some times even as but one of the many picturesque elements of Highland life."* J. & E. Pennell, *Our Journey to the Hebrides,* 1890. [Real Photographic postcard]

SKYE WOMAN WITH PEAT CREEL.

Broadford Temperance Hote

THIS HOTEL is close to the Pier, and commands a beautiful view of
Bay and surrounding Scenery. Magnificent Drives to Loch Coru
Sligachan, etc. Boots awaits all steamers from Oban, Mallaig, and Kyl
Lochalsh. **Terms Moderate, with every Home Comfort.**

POSTING. Boats and Fishing Free. Parties may supply their own Wi
MISS CAMPBELL, Proprietrix

BROADFORD HOTEL, SKYE.

E.1799.

24. The Broadford Hotel. Tradition has it that an inn was established here as early as 1611 by Lachlan MacKinnon of Strath, the only substance for which is the inscription "Established in 1611" set-up by a wishful landlord in the 19th century. The inn must have been impossibly crowded during the melee of the Broadford cattle fair. Indeed, a visitor in 1846 could take little delight in the place: *"I can bear it no longer, but must creep into my cotton-checked bed, and sleep, or weep, or get bitten by fleas, as the case may be."* [Real Photographic postcard by the Scholastic Souvenir Company of Blackpool, *circa* 1930]

25. The MacKinnon Memorial Hospital, Broadford, is a monument to a notable succession of ministers of Strath, son succeeding father for four generations from 1749 until 1888! The last incumbent was, *"Chairman of the School Board, road contractor, noted breeder of setters, a knowing judge of cattle, occupant of three large sheep farms, and, now verging on three-score, he preaches two sermons, one in Gaelic, the other in English, every Sunday.'* In the 1950s, the Health Board decided to enlarge the hospital to serve, not only the whole of Skye, but also the adjacent mainland. [A real photographic card by G.P. Abraham, F.R.P.S., of Keswick, a renowned mountain photographer]

MEDICINE CHESTS.

2292
MAHOGANY.

BATH CHAIR (WICKER) WITH WOOD FRAME.

35

26. Broadford Harbour and Mail Boat. Broadford was on the main west coast steamer route, and a central point for visitors wishing to view the Spar Cave, Elgol, Loch Coruisk and the Cuillins, *'the objects for which Skye is chiefly visited.'* Its origins as a township lie wholly within the 19th century, where, by 1840 there was, *"a good inn, two shops, a mill and a smithy ..... three markets are annually held for the sale of black-cattle and horses."* [Real Photographic Card from the Blackpool Scholastic Souvenir Company, *circa* 1932]

27. The Mailboat at Broadford. This shows the paddle-steamer 'Fusilier', a vessel of about 250 tons, built in 1888 for the Oban-Gairloch service. Like all MacBrayne steamers, she might be seen at various other locations and 'Fusilier' included Fort William, the Crinan Canal, Iona, Staffa and Ardrishaig during her long career. In 1931 she took over the Portree mail route from the 'Glencoe' for just one summer, and was here photographed leaving Broadford Pier. She was sold off in 1934 and eventually turned up off the Welsh coast, under her new name 'Lady Orme', sailing between Llandudno and the Menai Straits. She was scrapped in 1939. [Real Photographic postcard from the Blackpool Scholastic Souvenir Company, 1931]

Campbell's Hotel

BROADFORD

ISLE OF SKYE

Terms :—

Charabanc Tours

→8·□·8←

MONDAYS and FRIDAYS:

To ELGOLL for LOCH CORUISK... **4/6**

TUESDAYS and THURSDAYS:

To DUNVEGAN, *via* PORTREE,
and returning *via* STRUAN ... **12/-**

WEDNESDAYS:

To LOCH DHUGHAILL by OSTAIG,
calling at ORD on return journey **6/6**

Passengers may, if they desire, walk
round the coast from LOCH DHUGHAILL
and rejoin the 'bus at ORD. From these
two points an unique view is obtained of
the whole Coolin Range. It challenges
comparison with any other view in Skye.

SATURDAYS:

To QUIRAING, FLODDIGARRY
and UIG... ... ... **12/-**

28. Broadford Pier was the termination of the small railway line that ran from the marble quarries 3 miles away at Gilchrist. From here the marble was shipped to Europe until the quarry closed in 1913. Passenger steamers and puffers unloaded here, with goods awaiting collection being stored in a small building on the T-shaped end of the pier. With a revival in the small fishing industry (notably shellfish farming) the wheel has turned full circle, for the building on the right hand side of the pier is the old fishing station founded almost two centuries ago in a effort to stimulate a local industry. Campell's Hotel lies to the left. [Bromide from Valentine of Dundee]

19236 MILESTONE AT BROADFORD SKYE.

29. The year is 1937, and inclusive weekly terms in a good hotel are five guineas. Northern & Scottish Airways will fly you to Sollas on North Uist or direct from Renfrew to Glenbrittle in Skye. Main Post Offices opened their doors at 8.00a.m. and put up the shutters at 7.30p.m., six days a week.The Bank of Scotland, its deposits of £39.5 million controlled from The Mound, Edinburgh, had a branch at Armadale. At Broadford this milestone proclaimed to all that the people of Skye were very independent souls, being so far from the heart of Central Government! [Photographic card by Judges Ltd., Hastings, England]

30. *Beinn na Caillich* and Old Corry, Skye. Behind Broadford on the east coast of Skye, an extensive strath extends westwards across the island to the shore of Loch Slapin and Strathaird. Since the 13th century, it was the heartland of the Clan MacKinnon until 1789 when Strathaird was sold to Alexander MacAlister, renowned for most cruelly driving tenants from their homes to make way for sheep. This tranquil scene of a crofting family making hay stands in contrast to the ugly memories of their parents' day. In the middle distance lies Old Corry, the *'Coirechatachan'* where Johnson and Boswell were hosted by MacKinnon, and had such a cheerful time. In the distance lies *Beinn na Caillich* (hill of the Old Woman). At its crest is a cairn said to cover the remains of a Scandinavian Princess buried here, *"so that the winds of her native land might play around her final resting place".* [Unattributed real photographic card]

31. White Marble Quarry, Gilchrist, Broadford. As early as 1773, Dr. Johnson had speculated that *"perhaps by diligent search in this world of stone, some reliable species of marble might be discovered".* In 1824, John MacCulloch waxed lyrical about the copious quantity of marble so evidently available. The quarry was extensively worked during the latter half of the 19th century, with marble used as far afield as the altar in Iona Cathedral. This miniature railway was constructed to transport material to a pier at Broadford. Many of those shown in this 1904 view could neither understand Gaelic nor English being migrant Belgians or Frenchmen brought in for their particular skills in cutting and working the marble. An attempt to resurrect the industry in 1907 eventually failed, and the old workings near *Cille Chriosd* were abandoned in 1913. [Hand-coloured postcard 'Made in Saxony' and overprinted 'for MacInnes, Post Office, Broadford, Skye']

32 & 33. The Red Hills from Torrin. A casual scatter of black houses across a mosaic of crofting land is here dominated by the rounded peaks of the Red Hills. The subdued form of these acid rocks contrasts strongly with the coarser and hard-grained gabbro and granites of Blaven in the Cuillins. [Original 1875 sepia prints from George Washington Wilson, Photographer Royal in Scotland]

34. The township of Torrin, taken from virtually the same spot as the previous view. This latter view was taken in the 1950s and as such strictly speaking lies outside our remit. It is included here simply to show what changes were taking place, even within such a short span of years, in places so seemingly removed as this. [Full colour postcard from J. Arthur Dixon Ltd]

35. 'The island of Rhum from Elgol.' This card underlines the proximity of the islands, one to another. It also reinforces what eludes many visitors who arrive only by crossing the narrows from Kyle or Glenelg, that for centuries the sea has been the main highway uniting those settled around its margins. [J.B.White of Dundee.'Best of All' series.]

The Gas Chrom or Crooked Spade, Skye

36. *"Although the crofting system was in many respects baneful and injurious, yet it had the perceptible advantage of improving the aspect of the country, as each crofter, by having a small allotment for himself, was anxious to turn it to the best account, which could not be effected by the old run-rig system."* Rev. John Mackinnon, 2nd Statistical Account. [Coloured, printed postcard with the mark G.W.W., postmarked 1911]

37. Elgol is the last township on the Strathaird peninsula and where most visitors turn their cars for the pleasant return to Broadford. It is also in the summer months a point of departure for small boats taking visitors across to the head of Loch Slapin to visit Loch Coruisk. *"Saw a most wonderful sunset over the Coolins last night."* is the brief but stirring message carried on this particular card. [J.B.White of Dundee, ' Best of All' Series]

38. A striking card of Elgol school and schoolhouse against a backdrop of Loch Scavaig and the Cuillin. Surely such a setting will in itself have worked a potent force on a young child's imagination. [J.B.White of Dundee.'Best of All' series: Reproduced here by kind permission of the Clan Donald Lands Trust]

THE GRAND VIEW TEA ROOMS. ELGOL. SKYE

39. The *'Grand View Tea Rooms'* at Elgol on the shore of Loch Scavaig. More interest might be attached to the small wooden hut on the slope to the right of the picture. At the mouth of Loch Scavaig lies the island of Soay, a little over 2,500 acres in extent and occupied by several families. In the 1930s, and after several disasters, the islanders petitioned for a direct telegraphic link with Skye. Dame Flora MacLeod, the Landlord, and the Secretary of State took up the case with the Post Office, and in December, after much foot-dragging by the Post Office, the link was established *via* this small shed. The burden of the cost of running the transmitter was shared between various Government departments, Skye District Council and Dame Flora MacLeod. The first message transmitted by the islanders was to their M.P. - *"The inhabitants of Soay greet you by radio link to express their appreciation of your efforts on their behalf".* [An unattributed card, *circa* 1941]

TOUR 3   The Cuillin
(including Loch Coruisk) to Sligachan

40. An Edwardian party alights from the 'S.S. Glencoe' at Loch Scavaig, undoubtedly to visit Loch Coruisk. The rowing boat in the foreground is the 'Loch Scavaig'. MacBrayne's official guide for the summer tours describes the route from Mallaig to this loch and assures passengers that *"after anchoring we are landed in large and comfortable boats on the estate of Strathaird".* [A card from the MacIntyre's Series, Fort William; the photographer is credited by his initials, 'D.K.,' only]

For . . .

Holidays and Health

.. 'NO PLACE CAN ..
COMPARE WITH THE

WESTERN HIGHLANDS &
ISLANDS OF SCOTLAND.

BRACING AIR.   GRAND VARIED SCENERY.
A LAND FULL OF HISTORIC INTEREST.

510   AT ELGOL SHORE, ISLE OF SKYE

41. "...on turning a point, such a scene broke suddenly on the view as seemed to overwhelm the mind with awe, surprise and rapture. We were entering a narrow loch, enclosed on either side by rocks of enormous height, which formed, as it were, the portal to a region of wonders, filled with the most astonishing forms that even fancy could devise. Everywhere before us rose peaks and points and pinnacles, jagged and serrated and taking the wildest possible shapes, ...Immediately about us was rock, rock, rock; everywhere perfectly bare, black herbless rock, ...huge smooth swells of wondrous breadth of surface, to an altitude which, being immediately over our heads, it is no exaggeration to say the eye ached in measuring." Rev. Chauncy Hare Townsend, 1846. [Kyle Pharmacy Series]

18746. THE BOAT LANDING. LOCH CORUISK. SKYE. INVERNESS.

42. The Boatlanding, Loch Coruisk. "*To reach the upper end of Lock Scavaig, at the nearest point to Loch Coruisk, will occupy the tourist about three hours from the time of leaving the Spar Cave. In the bosom of the majestic solitude before him, and only about a quarter of a mile from the landing-place, reposes the far-famed Loch Coruisk. It is approached along the course of the brawling stream which discharges the superfluous waters of Loch Coruisk into Loch Scavaig.*" From Black's *Picturesque Tourist*, 1851. [Judges' Ltd. Hastings]

43. Coiruisk (*caoir' uisge*: the corry of water, or cauldron). The most remarkable loch in Britain: -
"The dead, dull lake lay beneath; the ruins, as it were, of a former world were scattered on all sides; and above, as far as the eye can pierce through the murky clouds, rose the vast rocky pinnacles, their extremest heights obscured at intervals, when we could behold the grim and awful giants keeping their eternal watches. There was nothing within the visible diurnal sphere that breathed the breath of life - no sound, nor the sight of any moving thing - nothing but dead and stony, seemingly, a God-forsaken world. We almost longed, in this cloud-capped, thunder-stricken region, to hear the voice of gladsome bird, or even of murmuring bee - but all, so far as regarded living nature, was silent as the grave. The whole scene from first to last exceeded in its sterile grandeur whatever had previously been seen in this, perhaps in any other country". James Wilson,1842. [Printed card from a watercolour by L.M.Long, Polytechnic Series]

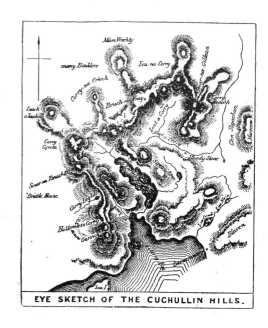

EYE SKETCH OF THE CUCHULLIN HILLS.

A Skye Crofter's Home, near Sligachan.   Abrahams' Series. No. 45. Keswick.

44. A Skye Crofter's Home, near Sligachan. "*A well-to-do house probably has a window at the end where the family live. ...A misty gleam streams through the opening, by which the smoke ought to escape, but the interior is chiefly dependent for light on the ever-open doorway. To enable the door thus to do double work, it is generally made in two halves, the lower half being frequently closed, while the upper half stands open. If you approach such a dwelling, a kindly voice will assuredly bid you welcome in the Gaelic tongue, (for they "have no English"), and as you stoop to enter the low doorway, you become aware that the peat-reek which saturates the thatch, likewise fills the interior of the house with a dense blue cloud, stinging and choking to unaccustomed eyes and lungs. Then you perceive that half of the house is devoted to the cattle - is, in fact, the byre, and a very dirty byre to boot.*" Mrs. Cummings, author of '*A Home in Fiji*', '*A Lady's Cruise in a French Man-of-War*', etc. etc. 1886 Edinburgh. [Abrahams' Series, No. 45. Keswick]

81. The Crack Slab

45. *"At a recent meeting of this club, the excellent president drew the attention of the members to certain peaks of continental mountains deemed inaccessible, but here, according to the Admiralty surveyor, is one in the British Isles, never trodden by the foot of man. Surely some bold member of the Club will scale this Skye peak ere long, and tell us that it was but a stroll before breakfast."* Charles Richard Weld,*'Two Months in the Highlands, Orcadia, and Skye'* 1860. [Photographic postcard by G.P. Abraham, F.R.P.S. of Keswick. Reproduced here by kind permission of the Clan Donalds Lands Trust]

The Inaccessible Pinnacle. Sgurr Dearg.
Near the Sligichan Inn.   "The Rock-climbing centre Par Excellence of
(Isle of Skye)   the British Isles" (See Badminton - Page 342)

Abraham's Series, Keswick

46. *"We get lots of grand climbing up here and a great selection of weather, some days splendid, and others dripping. We've not climbed the rock on the picture and are very ambitious to do so. G.R.D."* August, 1908. The message says it all. [Black and white printed card by Abraham's of Keswick]

47. The Sligachan Hotel in the 1870s with the peak of Marsco as a backcloth. At the time this photograph was taken, Skye was gaining an enviable reputation as one of the most popular climbing centres in Europe. The Cuillin contains many of the Scottish pinnacles over 3000ft, known collectively as "Munros" (after Sir Hugh Munro who listed them), attracting such eminent climbers as Professor James Forbes, G.P. Abraham, F.S. Smythe, George Mallory and Skye's own John MacKenzie of Sconser. [Sepia photograph from the George Washington Wilson studio.]

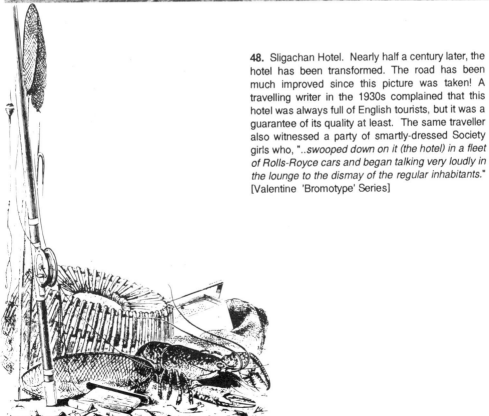

48. Sligachan Hotel. Nearly half a century later, the hotel has been transformed. The road has been much improved since this picture was taken! A travelling writer in the 1930s complained that this hotel was always full of English tourists, but it was a guarantee of its quality at least. The same traveller also witnessed a party of smartly-dressed Society girls who, "..*swooped down on it (the hotel) in a fleet of Rolls-Royce cars and began talking very loudly in the lounge to the dismay of the regular inhabitants.*" [Valentine 'Bromotype' Series]

49. A postcard entitled, 'Taking Home Peats for the Fire'. Similar cards were produced for many of the Outer Hebrides, but it is unusual to see a man carrying the peat. Most of the time the women did this particular chore, whilst the men did the digging. But this very 'posed' photograph shows Donald Murchison of Woodend, Portree, alias *Domhnall na Coille* (Donald of the wood), the postman for the Glenmore district who had previously been photographed for a card showing him in his 'postman' role. Now, the photographer simply removed Donald's post-bag and walking-stick to produce yet another, 'character' postcard. [Black and white printed postcard produced in the 1930s by Valentine of Dundee]

50. A typical Hebridean postcard sold from the early 1900s onward, although the photograph was taken in the 1880s before such postcards were legally available to the British public. Many early postcard publishers relied upon older material to satisfy the demands of the sophisticated traveller coming from a town that had telephones, electric light and the motor car. This is just the sort of postcard they wanted to post home with the usual, *'Isn't it quaint'* type of message. Thankfully we know the identities of both of these men; John Martin, seated, is talking to *Calum Chaluim* (Calum son of Calum) at Fisherfield by Portree. In his younger days, Calum had been the turnkey of the gaol at Portree and, it is alleged, took his prisoners with him when lifting the peats. [George Washington Wilson photograph reproduced as a black and white printed postcard *circa* 1902]

51. The harbour at Portree in the 1870s from Cuddy Point. The original design was by Thomas Telford, but changes were underway. Douglas Row had yet to be extended to the left to form Quay Street, and the thin woodland on the slopes above, cleared to make way for the Skye Gathering Hall. The solitary white building was at this time no longer in use as the gaol while below, and at the foot of the bank leading up into the town, stands the ice-house. This is a relic from the days when the harbour was once so dense with fishing smacks that it was possible to walk across the harbour without getting your feet wet. Indeed, until the advent of trawlers in the 1880s, as many as 800 boats went out from this harbour to the herring. To the right is Beaumont Crescent, a terrace of eight houses built in 1839 and advertised as, *"neatly furnished, and well adapted for respectable families."* [An original George Washington Wilson photograph]

52. In the Summer of 1889, Dr. Francis Gray Smart, together with his wife, Marion, a servant and a maid, set off on a tour of Scotland. From Gairloch they embarked on the paddle steamer 'Mountaineer', arriving at Portree harbour sometime between 7.00a.m. and 7.30a.m. This view of the bare quayside, together with other remarkable photographs, were to lie hidden for over 90 years within the faded covers of a photographic album, until their re-discovery in 1986. Exactly a century after setting-up the camera on the deck to take this single view of the harbour, it appeared as a postcard. [Produced by Firtree Publishing Ltd. Fort William, 1989]

SKYE LASSIES.

53. Cutting seaweed at the *Sgurr Dubh* (Black Rock), Portree, below Ben Chracaig, the traditional homelands of Clan Nicolson. The seaweed would be carried to the fields in baskets by the women and worked into soil freshly tilled with the *cas chrom*. [Real photographic postcard by Valentine of Dundee, *circa* 1902]

54. More *'Skye Crofters'* on a black and white printed postcard posted in 1915, to a lady in Sheffield, and carrying the message, "*This is the sort of thing we feast our eyes on.*" It should be remembered that there would be a certain 'culture-shock' for the sophisticated 'townie' meeting the black-house inhabitants at this time. Yet in 1915, when this card was being written by a summer visitor, young Skye-men were in France and Flanders, destined never to return to the family croft. One coloured version of this card carries the name *'Miss MacArthur, Portree .'* Was this the name of the woman at the spinning wheel or perhaps rather the name of the local outlet for this card? [Black and white printed card from the W.R.&S. 'Reliable Series', William Ritchie and Sons, publishers in Edinburgh]

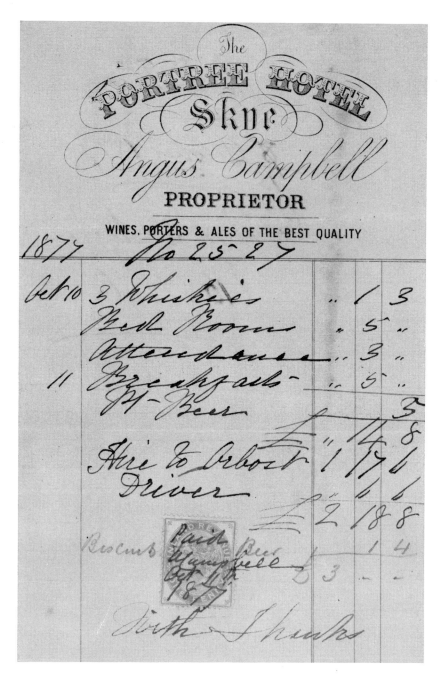

A little piece of ephemera; the Portree Hotel bill of a Mr. Forbes, submitted as part of his claim for expenses after a trip to Skye in October, 1877. The total claimed was £15.2.6d (written on the back of this bill), but at the hotel on 10th October, 1877, he and a companion drank three whiskies at 5d each, and retired to their rooms, numbers 25 and 27, which cost 8/- because they had 'attendance'. The following morning, after breakfast, they hired a carriage and driver to take them to Orbost, near Dunvegan, at a total cost of £2.4.0d. Added to the bill, and written in pencil across the stamp, are the words, 'Biscuits and Beer 1/4d'. Perhaps their lunch on the road to Orbost?

Somerlead Square, Portree, Skye

55. Somerled Square, Portree, capital of the district. The square takes its name from the 12th century warrior chief and progenitor of the MacDonalds. The medley of buildings here (*circa* 1903) testify to the rapid development of the township during the 19th century, especially pronounced as it became the acknowledged centre for professional businesses such as banks, solicitors, agents etc. The Portree Hotel was built in 1875 to cater for this increase in traffic while Wentworth Street, leading to the descent to the harbour, at this time could boast 16 grocer shops! Though you would not think it to be so busy from this view. [Tinted card, 'Made in Saxony' and overprinted for 'J.W. Dickson, Portree']

Somerled Square, Portree.   753/20

56. Merely turning the camera 180 degrees produces this view of the western side of Somerled Square, Portree. The large building on the left was built in 1873 as the Caledonian Bank, (now the Bank of Scotland). Beyond is the Episcopalian church of St. Columba, one of the *"architectural beauties"* of Skye and completed in 1883. Just a spire and a steady issue of worshippers betrays the presence of the United Free Presbyterian church. Could the photographer have *dared* to take this picture on the Sabbath? [Black and white printed card from the, 'W.R.&S. Reliable Series', William Ritchie and Sons, publishers in Edinburgh; *circa* 1908]

N. BEATON,

PIER GARAGE, PORTREE

**Sole Accredited Dealer for MORRIS CARS
in Isle of Skye.**

OFFICIAL REPAIRER TO A.A.

AGENT FOR AUSTIN, HILLMAN, and BEAN CARS;
TRIUMPH and ARIEL MOTOR CYCLES

MOTOR BOAT FOR HIRE ANY PERIOD.

Neil Beatons Garage advertised in Kenneth MacRae's *'Handbook and Guide to the "Misty Isle" of Skye.' 1921.*

57. Somerled Square, Portree on a wet weekday. The North of Scotland Bank to the left across the square, with the Bank of Scotland centre right. Perhaps not an unusual occurrence even for the 1930s. [Real Photographic card]

Royal Hotel, Portree

58. On 1st July, 1746 and in pouring rain Flora MacDonald and Prince Charles Edward Stuart made their way from Kingsburgh to Portree where they arrived at Charles MacNab's Inn thoroughly drenched. After changing his kilt the Prince had a dram, a meal, *'and expressed the desire to stay all night.'* They stayed only two hours whereupon Prince Charles repaid Flora the half-crown he owed her, told her he hoped he might yet meet with her at the Court of St. James's, then strode down to the shore where a boat was waiting to carry him to Raasay. In time a far grander building replaced MacNab's small establishment, and also a change of name in honour of its memorable patron. [Valentine of Dundee, postmarked 1924]

The Schools, Portree.

59. Following the introduction of compulsory education through the 1872 Education Act, work was started on a new school at Portree to serve the educational needs of Skye children. The building was opened in 1875 and 30 years later, upgraded in status to a Higher Grade School. At this time there were some 250 students and 15 teachers giving instruction in Latin, Greek, French, Maths, History, Art and Gaelic. Sadly, the fine old buildings were demolished in 1971. Without any concession to its island setting, the regional Authority imposed a ponderous suburban horror upon the community which, 20 years later, still remains uncompleted and in a sadly deteriorated condition. [Black and white printed card from the 'W.R.&S. Reliable Series' William Ritchie and Sons, publishers in Edinburgh; *circa* 1900]

Young Salts, Portree Bay.
RELIABLE SERIES

60. 'Young Salts, Portree Bay'. Posted by 'Ella' to Miss Katie Cant, daughter of a shoemaker who lived in Belmont Street, Newtyle, Forfarshire (a village famous in Victorian times for its artificial manure!). The sender writes, *"On this card you will see five of my school companions. We are getting very wet weather just now. We are all well but Baby is fearful cross, always crying. I fell into the Bay once but was not drowned."* What good fortune! [Black and white printed card from the 'W.R.&S. Reliable Series', William Ritchie and Sons, Publishers in Edinburgh; *circa* 1902]

ELGIN HOSTEL FOR BOYS, PORTREE, SKYE.

61. The Elgin Hostel for Boys, Portree was one of four school hostels provided by the Carnegie Trust for scholars attending the secondary schools at Stornoway and Portree. Named after the Earl of Elgin & Kincardine, Chairman of the Trust since 1923, the building was opened by the Duke and Duchess of York on September 12th, 1933. It provided accommodation for 40 boys, a matron, two resident masters, a cook and four maids, and future planners might take guidance from the fact that its elegant design was, *"suggested by 18th and 19th century farm-steadings, country houses, and cottages, which, with their harled and white-washed walls and slated roofs, seem so unobtrusive and at home in a Highland setting."* [Real Photographic postcard by the Scholastic Souvenir Company of Blackpool]

62. Cattle market showing travellers tents at Sluggans, on the west side of Portree. Since 1580, there was a twice-yearly fair held here. In the 18th and 19th centuries these became busier as drovers from the lowlands came in search of stock to feed a growing population. Such fairs were a magnet to the 'Travellers' or 'Tinkers', whose knowledge of stock, and horses in particular, was unrivalled. This was a time for Skye folk to get their pots and pails replaced or mended, and many a tin can was handed to one of these wizards to be returned as a smart milk jug! [Black and white printed card from the 'W.R.&S'. 'Reliable Series' of William Ritchie and Sons, publishers in Edinburgh; *circa* 1905. Bears the retailer's name, 'D. MacPherson, Kyleakin, Skye']

TOUR 5   Around the Trotternish Ridge

63. *"For some years after the construction of roads the common people would not on any account travel on them. They said that the stones and gravel both bruised their feet and wore their shoes, and they preferred to follow the old paths, uneven and boggy as they were"* (Rev. A. Clerk, 2nd Statistical Account, 1841). Just half a century later the state of the road from Portree north to Staffin before the improvements of 1914 might indeed justify such a view. [Real Photograph]

64. The "*Cas Choom*", Skye. At least as early as the 17th century, a particular type of agricultural instrument, the *cas chrom,* or foot plough was in use in the North West Highlands and Islands of Scotland. Essentially a form of spade, it consists of a curved shaft leading to a crook or angle, the end of which carries an iron shoe. There is a peg set in the shaft, just above the crook which allows the user to push the blade into the earth, then jerking the lever arm, both raise the soil and cast it to the right. It is an instrument ideally suited to peaty or rocky soils, its power of leverage, particularly handy in removing rocks and boulders. It was shown in 1811 that 12 men could turn an acre in a day with the *cas chrom,* and on land where no plough could be used, even had the crofters been able to afford one! [Valentine Series, *circa* 1900]

65. Approaching Staffin Bay from the south the former long rectangular crofting strips are still in clear evidence radiating away from the water margin. Just over a century ago the mill here was often busy all day and night grinding meal from 'the granary of Skye' as Trottemish was once known. In 1883 armed marines stationed in Staffin Lodge were given additional protection from the verbal scorn of the crofters by a warship stationed in the bay. [J.B.White of Dundee 'Best of All' series]

66. Flodigarry Hotel in the shadows of the Trottemish Ridge, sometime in the late 1930s. An advertisement for this hotel in a 1932 guide suggested that the hotel, *"recently converted from a mansion known as Flodigarry House to a well appointed hotel"* was, *"the home of Flora MacDonald after her marriage."* The mansion however, was only completed in 1895, sadly just a little too late for Flora to enjoy the hospitality of its first owner, Alexander Livingston MacDonald. [Photographic sepia postcard by Judges Ltd. of Hastings]

Flora mcdonald

Flora Macdonald's Cottage, Flodigarry, Skye

67. Adjacent to the Flodigarry Hotel is the cottage where, in 1751, Flora MacDonald came to live with her husband, Allan MacDonald. Five of their seven children were born here over the following eight years, whereupon Allan and Flora returned to live at Kingsburgh. By 1948, the owner of the hotel had changed his advertisement to read, *"In the cottage adjoining the hotel lived Flora MacDonald, preserver of Bonnie Prince Charlie, the outstanding heroine of the 1745 adventure."* [Real photographic card]

68. Entitled, *'Skye Crofters'* and photographed sometime in the latter half of the 19th century, it tells an obvious tale of hardship for this crofting family. Certainly, the sides of their house could do with a trim! [Black and white, produced in Germany in the early 1900's, and bearing the imprint 'Maclaines Series Postcards']

69

HANDLOOM WEAVING.

69. *"Another industry lost* (to Trotternish) *is weaving. There were quite a number of weavers. The women were busy teasing and carding the wool, and spinning it into thread. When the web was got from the weaver, the waulking* (shrinking of the cloth) *was done. Waulking was a great attraction for lads and lassies, who joined in the waulking songs. At the end was a scramble for the* mnathan luaidh, *each lad endeavouring to get his own favourite to see her home."* William Mackenzie, *Skye: Iochdar - Trotternish.* 1930. [Unattributed postcard printed at about the turn of the century]

Duntulm Castle as it stood in the later 19th century.

70. Duntulm Castle, Kilmuir, formerly a MacLeod stronghold and, until 1730, home to the MacDonald chiefs. One of the last photographs to show the Keep, which thereafter collapsed in a heap, leaving only the central, subsidiary tower to give some visual height to the complex, until it too fell in the gales of 1990. [A 'Herald Series' postcard produced by W. Holmes & Co. of Glasgow in the 1920s]

71. View from the ruins of Duntulm Castle in 1929 showing part of the castle now fallen. Tradition relates that the castle was formerly the residence of a Norse chief, David, at a time when the western seaboard was under the rule of Norway. Duntulm was thereafter occupied by the MacLeods until ousted by the MacDonalds in 1482. The tussle for possession of the castle, (and thereby of the district of Trotternish itself) consumed much of the energies of these two families during the following century. The castle was reputedly haunted by the ghost of *Donald Gorm Mor*, who, with the help of two companions, would nightly walk the undervaults, helping themselves to the drink stored there! ['Real Photograph' from Valentine of Dundee]

72. Free Church and School, Kilmuir. [Real Photographic card]

73. 'A Skye Crofter's Home' is the caption to this 1920s postcard, although the actual picture was taken in the early 1880s. Two elderly men sit behind the black-house; one makes a creel whilst the other watches. On the roof of the hut is a broken towel-rail, probably discarded by some local hotel-keeper, but retained by the crofter for some future use. Black-houses were still occupied after the end of the Second World War, although the 1948 edition of the Official Guide to Skye assured the visitor that *"these primitive dwellings are being replaced by up-to-date cottages."* [Originally produced as a sepia photograph by George Washington Wilson in the 1880s but here reproduced as a real photographic postcard in the 'Camden Series', issued in the 1920s]

THE ROYAL MAIL IN SKYE.

74. About the year 1730, Duntulm Castle was abandoned to become a quarry for a new MacDonald residence at Monkstadt, 8km to the south. It was here, within the first twelve months of occupation, that Lady Margaret gave birth to their first son James, heir to the chiefdom. A cardinal who interviewed him reported to the Pope, " *I addressed him in seven different languages, and he answered me in all with fluency and obvious familiarity; and when I was about to leave the room he gave an order to his servant in a language that I am sure nobody in the world understands but themselves.*" - he was of course referring to Gaelic. [Valentine's 'Bromotype' Series]

75. Uig Bay, today the gateway to the Western Isles, courtesy of Caledonian MacBrayne, but here as it looked in the 1880s. The picturesque tranquility belies the heavy oppressions of a rack-renting landlord, Capt. Fraser who, in just one year, had raised rents here by 30%. The Uig flood of October, 1877 which swept away his home and Estate Manager, was regarded by many as divine judgement upon the man. [Issued as a photograph from the studio of George Washington Wilson in the 1880s, but here reproduced as a black and white print with the imprint of J.G. MacKay, Portree; *circa* 1902]

76. Uig fishing industry. Since the 18th century successive governments had pinned their hope upon the sea as offering a solution to to the economic problems bedevilling a part of the kingdom otherwise disadvantaged from industrial development. There was widespread belief that the best solution to the problem lay in stimulating a fishing industry. However, the tax on salt necessary to cure the fish initially hampered development, while the capricious movements of the herring shoals eventually confounded all hopes. Into the early decades of the 20th century many a small 'industry' was run as this one at Uig, sending many a barrel of fine west coast herring to England and the continent. Today, contrary to the visitors expectation, fresh locally-caught fish is not easy to obtain in the shops. [Real photographic postcard *circa* 1910]

75

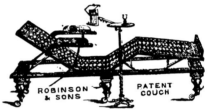

77. A superb photographic postcard dating from the first decade of the century, showing the John Martin Hospital at Uig. Opened in 1905, it survived for almost 60 years and many bouncing babies born here are fit Skye men and women today! A fire destroyed the building after it was closed down, and a youth hostel now occupies the site. ['British Made' real photographic card, *circa* 1920]

TOUR 6   To Dunvegan and Glendale

78. 'Farewell to the Old Homestead, Isle of Skye' is the title of this 1920s card, an ambigious title in view of the emotive emigration of crofters the century before. Here however, it might be taken simply as a bovine lament at being driven away to market prior to the long drove south. In the background is Bernisdale schoolhouse, and by a distant telegraph pole, a small knot of children are waiting to see the herd pass by. [A Real Photograph by J.B. White Ltd. Dundee]

79. Gesto Hospital was founded in the 1850s by Kenneth MacLeod of Greshornish (died 1869), who had made his fortune as an indigo planter in India. This was the first hospital on the island, though latterly it was used for geriatric patients. [Real Photographic postcard from the Scholastic Souvenir Company of Blackpool, *circa* 1930]

DUNVEGAN CASTLE

Prologue.

A S I sat painting on the open moor,
Above Dunvegan's loch and winding shore,
Above the rolling wood of larch and fir,
Whose plumèd tops the western breezes stir,
E'en as I drank the music of the wood,
The pastoral sounds, which marked the varying mood
Of man and pratt'ling child, of beast and bird,
Or clatt'ring hoofs of horses crisply heard;
As fell mine eye upon that castle old
With all its company of isles untold,
Peering beyond, to where in open sea
Blue hills of Harris loomed transparently;

....

by Harold Steward Rathbone
1900

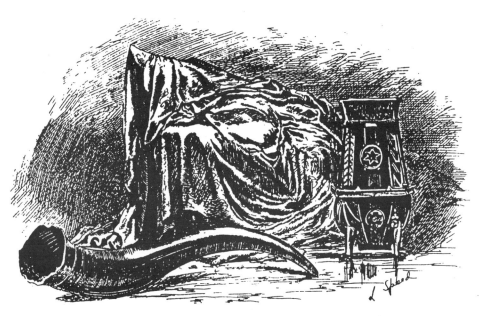

HORN.

80. Perhaps the most famous of all Hebridean castles, Dunvegan Castle has been in continuous occupation by just one family, the MacLeods, since the early 13th century. A succession of post-medieval additions have greatly altered its earlier character, yet maintaining its strongly defensive aspect. Dunvegan Castle is perhaps as equally renowned for its relics; Rory Mor's Drinking Horn, the Dunvegan Cup, and the *Bratach Sith* or Fairy Flag. The latter, a tattered piece of faded silk, reputedly given to Iain, the fourth chief, by a fairy wife as a protection for the Clan. More recent examination however, indicates an origin in the East where it might have been obtained as a holy relic. [Black and white printed postcard from the W.R.&S. 'Reliable Series', William Ritchie and Sons, publishers in Edinburgh; posted in 1911]

81. The 27th Chief of MacLeod, Sir Reginald MacLeod, on the battlements of Dunvegan Castle in the early 1930s. In 1929, he succeeded his brother, Norman Magnus to the title, and in September 1933 he entertained the Duke and Duchess of York at the Castle. Sadly he died the following year and his daughter took the title, 'Flora, Mrs. MacLeod of MacLeod'. [Real photographic card]

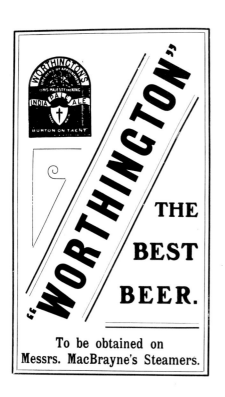

"WORTHINGTON"

THE
BEST
BEER.

To be obtained on
Messrs. MacBrayne's Steamers.

DUNVEGAN HOTEL, DUNVEGAN, SKYE.

82. The burgeoning tourist trade of the 1920s and 1930s encouraged the hotel trade to promote their establishments by way of illustration. Here, the Dunvegan hotel also subtly reveals its suitability for the motorist, offering also the convenience of a 'HOTEL GA(RAGE)' just behind the tea-room. Its former dignity now lies concealed behind a lean-to. [Blackpool Scholastic Souvenir Company]

HIGHLAND CATTLE SALE, LONMORE, DUNVEGAN, SKYE.

83. A great little picture but not, perhaps a best seller with the general public! The Blackpool Scholastic Souvenir Company again. *"Twinkly-eyed cattle-buyers in brown knickerbockers and brown caps"*, is author S.P.B. Mais's 1934 description of the men who travelled from the mainland for these Skye sales. This particular cattle sale at Lonmore, Dunvegan was photographed in the early 1930s when a cow in-calf fetched £11.5.0d in Skye. Perhaps the cattle-men themselves were the buyers of such postcards, reporting their progress and purchases to those at home. [Photographic card from the Blackpool Scholastic Souvenir Company]

84. Native and his grandson, Skye. *'Nowhere are
the little ones more deeply cared for, and more
heartily welcomed. Poor though the hearth may be
that house is reckoned poorest where the quiver is
empty, for the Highlanders say that a home without
the voices of children is dreary as a farm without
sheep or kye.'* Mrs Cummings, 1886. [Real
photographic card, postmarked 1904]

CÀRN CUIMHNE CLANN MHIC CRUIMEIN
A BHA O DHUALACHAS NÀM PÌOBAIREAN AIC MACLEÒID
FAD DHEICH CINEALACH
ACUS A BHA CLIÙITEACH AIRSON DEILBH IS CLUICH
IS TEACASC CIÙIL MHÓIR
IS ANN DLÙTH AIR AN LÀRAICH SO
A BHA SCOIL CHIÙIL MHIC CRUIMEIN
1500 - 1800, A.D.

85. The MacCrimmon Memorial, Borreraig. Hereditary pipers to the MacLeods since the 16th century, their college at Galtragill drew aspiring pipers from throughout Western Europe. Indeed, "*no man was considered a finished piper until he had studied at the MacCrimmon College.*" Sometime around 1670, the college removed to Borreraig until its closure a century later. In 1933 a stone cairn was raised on the site, its inscription reads: "The Memorial Cairn of the MacCrimmons of whom ten generations were the hereditary pipers of MacLeod and who were renowned as composers, performers and instructors of the classical music of the bagpipe. Near to this post stood the MacCrimmon's School of Music, 1500-1800." ['Best of All Series', J.B. White Ltd., Dundee]

The Lighthouse, Glendale, Skye.

86. The Lighthouse here at Neist Point is without doubt the most dramatically situated around this island's coastline. It was quite new when this photograph was taken, built to a design by David. A. Stevenson, Engineer to the Northern Lighthouse Board. Note one of the lighthouse keepers to the left. The range of buildings at the rear are largely accommodation with store houses and engine housing in separate buildings at the lower end of the compound. In 1989 the lighthouse was automated and most of the buildings sold. [A black and white printed postcard carrying the overprint of H. MacDonald, Stationer, Oban]

87. Pooltiel Bay, Glendale, with the entrance to Hamara Lodge to the left. During the winter of 1882-3 crofters' grievances welled up into organised resistance to landlord oppression. The landlords were driven to appeal to the authorities and an attempt was made to station a sergeant and three constables here at Hamara Lodge. They were set upon and ejected, as was a messenger-at-arms the following day. On January 20th,1883, several hundred men and women marched on Dunvegan to drive the police out of the district. This brought matters to a head, and, on February 9th, a gunboat of marines landed one Malcolm MacNeill, a Poor Law official, on the shore at Pooltiel in a last attempt to find a peaceful solution to the situation. By persuading four of the five ringleaders to appear before the justices at Edinburgh, a more tragic outcome was avoided. [Unattributed black and white printed postcard]

Orbost Hotel
Near DUNVEGAN
ISLE OF SKYE

THE HOTEL, having 6,000 acres of Glens and Moorland, is beautifully situated with magnificent sea and mountain views. Very Sporting Private 9-Hole Golf Course, charge per round, 1/- Safe bathing from sandy beach. Excellent Sea Fishing, boats and tackle provided free for visitors' use. Tennis, Putting Course, Indoor Tennis, Shooting by arrangement.

" . . . . Had I the choice I should rather live at Orbost than at any other house in Skye. . . . ."
—ALEX. SMITH
in *A Summer in Skye.*

ORBOST HOTEL, by DUNVEGAN, ISLE OF SKYE.

E.1483

88. Orbost House began in the mid-18th century as a tack-house, thereafter undergoing a series of enlargements until around 1900 when it assumed its present form. Between the early 1930s and the end of the Second World War, the house was run as Orbost Hotel in succession to a 'drying-out' house for alcoholics. Residence for a week, inclusive of meals during the height of the season (July to October) was £5.5.0. The hotel boasted 6,000 acres of land, and a *"very sporting"* nine-hole golf course (one shilling per round!). Sea fishing, tennis, putting, and shooting (by arrangement) indicate the temptations on offer to entice the potential customer. Surprisingly, mains electricity was not installed until 1947. [Real Photographic card from the Scholastic Souvenir Company of Blackpool, *circa* 1934]

MAID OF THE CROFT.

WASHING WITH LUX, ROSKHILL RIVER, HARLOSH, SKYE.

E.1501.

89. Washing with Lux. Into the early years of the 20th century, washing was carried out by the burn-side. The water was heated in iron pots and poured into large tubs where, hitching up their skirts, the women would tramp amidst the clothes (hence the name 'trampers' or 'tramping'). Here by the side of the river at Harlosh the sheets are being wrung, with the 'Lux' barely visible above the bundle in the centre. [Real Photographic card from the Blackpool Scholastic Souvenir Company of Blackpool, *circa* 1932]

302. NIGHEADH PLAIDEACHAN SA CHAOL (A HIGHLAND WASHING AT KYLE.)

90. The more glamorous side of Washing Day. [Printed sepia postcard from the 'Kyle Pharmacy Series']

91. Kenneth, Joan and Ronnie Lamont pose for their photograph at Vatten School, *circa* 1925. [Unattributed. With thanks to all three for permission to reproduce this moment in their youth]

Minginish (Portnalong and Glenbrittle)

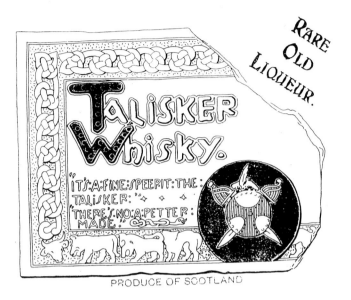

92. Talisker Distillery near Carbost was founded in 1830 by Hugh and Kenneth MacAskill, and visitors are still welcome (during certain hours in the tourist season), as they have been for over 160 years. *" ....of the only two manufactories established in the Isles, one is a good woollen factory at Portree, but the other is a distillery at Tallisker, in the Isle of Skye, which turns out fourty-five thousand gallons of whisky per annum, of which about twenty-thousand are consumed on the Isle of Skye itself."* Mrs Cummings, *In the Hebrides* 1883.{Holmes' Real Photo Series, *circa* 1908]

PACKING THE WOOL AT PORTNALONG, SKYE

93. In 1921 The Board of Agriculture was responsible for the resettlement of a large number of emigrants from Lewis, Harris and Scalpay as a community at Portnalong on the west coast of Skye. The influx was in two waves. Each family was given 15-20 acres, three cows and a share in the sheep grazing in an effort to preserve community identities,whilst establishing a sound tripartite economic foundation in crofting, fishing, and the weaving traditions as practised in the homelands of Lewis and Harris. The latter was, until relatively recently, a very distinctive feature of this part of Skye, with annual gatherings, or *Feilltean,* where weavers offered the year's work in tweed and hosiery for sale. In this card of the 1930s, the sheared wool is packed ready for washing. [Real Photographic card, carrying the over-print of D. MacIntyre, Stationer, Portree]

DYEING THE WOOL AT PORTNALONG SKYE

94. An iron pot and a peat fire were equipment sufficient for a Hebridean cottage dyeing industry. Indeed it has been suggested that tartan may have been the product of small pots allowing only a limited number of matching colours. Here the wool is being dyed in its raw unspun state. With only a moderately small pot in which to carry out the process this allowed more wool to be colour matched than by immersing the skein or the finished cloth. [Real photographic card, bearing the name of D.MacIntyre, Portree]

SPINNING THE WOOL AT PORTNALONG, SKYE

95 & 96. These rather posed situations reveal the sustained appeal to the postcard purchaser since George Washington Wilson's day of images showing the survival of relic traditions - what in another context might well be considered 'ethnic'. [Unattributed, but each bears the retailers name, 'D. MacIntyre, Stationer, Portree']

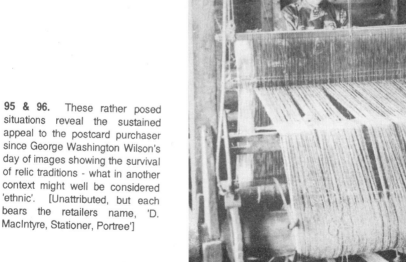

MAKING THE TWEED AT PORTNALONG, SKYE

1. Old Scotch plough.   2. *Caschroim*, or crooked spade.

HARVESTING IN GLEN BRITTLE, ISLE OF SKYE.

97. Following grievous injustices meted out to crofters and culminating in the land wars of the early 1880s the Crofters Act of June 1886 finally gave tenants security of tenure, the right to transfer land within the family, rights to compensation for improvement, and a land court with the power to fix fair rents - the Crofters Commission. These crofters would have been young children at the time their parents were struggling for the rights which they are seen here to be enjoying. [Unattributed postcard]

Glenbrittle Y.H., Skye. and Sgurr Bannachdich.

98. In 1934 the Scottish Youth Hostels Association commandeered the little schoolhouse here at Glen Brittle as a Youth Hostel. A few years later this was replaced with the smart new timber hostel shown here. In the 1930s and 1940s it had everything to attract the active visitor, boating, climbing, bathing and fishing. [Scottish Youth Hostel Series No. 141; postmarked early 1940s]

The joys of the open air

99. *"The walker who is interested in "old unhappy far-off things" will find much to his liking in Skye:....Boots are better than shoes if you intend to do much on the hills..... Skye is very wetting and a change of clothing is welcome. It will also add much to your comfort if you take some reliable anti-midge lotion with you, such as that recommended by the Scottish Tourist Board.'* B.H.Humble. *Tramping in Skye.* 1934. ['British Made' postcard, otherwise unattributed]

And so, homewards.

100. The journey ended our intrepid travellers prepare for the journey homewards. [Kyle Pharmacy Series]

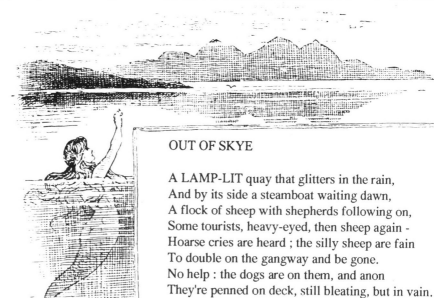

OUT OF SKYE

A LAMP-LIT quay that glitters in the rain,
And by its side a steamboat waiting dawn,
A flock of sheep with shepherds following on,
Some tourists, heavy-eyed, then sheep again -
Hoarse cries are heard ; the silly sheep are fain
To double on the gangway and be gone.
No help : the dogs are on them, and anon
They're penned on deck, still bleating, but in vain.

The daylight strengthens, and the sirens sound ;
The last rope splashes, and the engines churn ;
The quayside fades. O misty isle, it seems
As if no time to leave thee could be found
More fitting than the hour in which men turn
From sleeping, and, reluctant, lose their dreams.

J. F. Marshall.